LESSONS LEARNED

Poetry of the Vietnam War
and Its Aftermath

LESSONS LEARNED

Poetry of the Vietnam War
and Its Aftermath

Dale Ritterbusch

Viet Nam Generation, Inc. & Burning Cities Press

"Biogenesis" and "Words" were first anthologized in *Northwords*, The National Poetry Foundation, University of Maine at Orono, 1981.
"Search and Destroy" first appeared in *Carrying The Darkness*, Avon, New York, 1985. Republished in 1989 by Texas Tech University Press. W. D. Ehrhart, editor.
"A Matter of Fact: Nicaragua, 1983" appeared in *On The Street*, #9, Lakeside Press, Fall 1986.
"Choppers" appeared in *DEROS*, Vol. IV, No. 4, Sept. 1985.
"Shrapnel" appeared in *DEROS*, Vol. V, No. 2, March 1986.
"Canoe Trip," "After the War," "Winning Hearts and Minds," "Search and Destroy," "Better Dead Than Boring," and "A Matter of Fact: Nicaragua, 1983" were anthologized in *Eleven Wisconsin Poets*, Kendall-Hunt, 1987, first edition. The second edition of *Eleven Wisconsin Poets* was published in 1990.
"When It's Late," "Bien Hoa, 1968," "Conversation," and "Shoulders" appeared in *Nobody Gets Off the Bus*, The Viet Nam Generation, 1994.
"Night Ambush" appeared in *Calapooya Collage 18*, August, 1994.
"At the Crash Site of a B-52: January 1994" and "Search and Destroy" are scheduled to appear in *The Vietnam War in American Stories, Songs, and Poems*, Bedford-St. Martin's, H. Bruce Franklin, editor. (forthcoming 1995).

I wish to thank Bill Ehrhart for helping to sort through a manuscript accumulated over twenty-eight years. His suggestions for inclusion or rejection were invaluable; final responsibility, however, for determining which poems would be retained rests entirely with me.

Cover design: Steve Gomes. Cover photo: Dale Ritterbusch, taken on guard duty at Phuoc Vinh.

Copyright © 1995 by Dale Ritterbusch
All rights reserved
First printing
ISBN: 1-885215-08-8

White Noise No. 7

White Noise Poetry

David Connolly, *Lost in America* (No. 1)
Elliot Richamn, *Walk On, Trooper* (No. 2)
David Vancil, *The Homesick Patrol* (No. 3)
Gerald McCarthy, *Throwing the Headlines* (No.4)
Joe Amato, *Symptoms of a Finer Age* (No. 5)
M.L. Liebler, *Stripping the Adult Century Bare* (No. 6)
Dale Ritterbusch, *Lessons Learned* (No. 7)
Philip K. Jason, *The Separation: Poems* (No. 8)

Printed by Viet Nam Generation, Inc. & Burning Cities Press, 18 Center Road, Woodbridge, CT 06525. 203/387-6882; FAX: 203/389-6104. email: kalital@minerva.cis.yale.edu. SAN: 298-2412

*For Those Who Could Not
Put The War Behind Them*

CONTENTS

Part I

When It's Late	13
Geography Lesson	15
Choppers	16
Canoe Trip	18
Nothing To Be Afraid Of	20
The Somme	22
After the War	23
CBR	25
Entropy	28
To a Poet Who Disdains the Theme of War	29
Learning From One of My Laotian Students	30
The Right Thing To Do: Misocz, Ukraine, 1942	31
Carnage: Prologue	33
Taking the Easy Way	34

Part II

Night Tactics: Training Exercise With Water Moccasin	37
Search and Destroy	38
Winning Hearts and Minds	39
Interrogation	40
Bien Hoa, 1968	41
Night Ambush	42
Standard	44
GB	45
The Siamese Syph	47
Begging	48
Rolling Thunder	50
On the Gulf of Siam	51
Dust-Off	52
Bringing It In	53
Humpin' Through the Boonies	54
Why I Didn't Put In My Twenty	55

Commendation	56
Moving the Mines From Sattahip to Nakhon Phanom	57
Intelligence	58
Saigon, 1969	60
Not Getting It Right	61
Biogenesis	63
Words	65
Once Again	66
Pataya Beach R&R, 1968	67
Lessons Learned	68

Part III

Conversation	73
Back in the World	74
What There Is	76
Back in the Land of the Big PX	77
A Matter of Fact: Nicaragua, 1983	79
Boundary Waters	81
Confirmed	84
"A Beautiful Day For Bombing"	85
Nothing Personal	87
All That Returns	90
Hunting For Antiques	91
Taking Your Arm	92
Memorial Day, Quetico, 1980	94
A Good Day	95
To a Friend Who Still Insists on Writing About the War	97
For the Cameras	98
Follow Me	100
Shrapnel	101
Cambodia	102
Fishing For Bass	103
Marking Time	105
Moussorgsky, McGovern, Philadelphia	106
Night Ambush II	108

Interregnum	110
Better Dead Than Boring	111
Long After the War	113
At the Crash Site of a B-52: January 1994	115
How It Ends	116
Teaching the War	117
Friends	118
Shoulders	119
Wild Raspberries	120
Taps	121
Notes on the Poems	123

I.

*Be this the whetstone of your sword. Let grief
Convert to anger; blunt not the heart, enrage it.*

—Malcolm, *Macbeth* IV. iii. 228-229

WHEN IT'S LATE

Sometimes, when it's late
and the house is asleep
except for me
pacing from room to room,
I walk to the backyard,
look out across the ground
lit only
by a distant streetlamp.

I remember nights
in some Asian bar
drinking a few exotic beers
that sweat quickly
through the khaki's
heavy starch:

We'd walk out late
go back to the base
sleep off as much
of the war as we could.

When you were killed
I drank for days,
made love until I
couldn't recall
anything but the hot
sun, the red dust
rising.

Now, this late
under the circling stars
I see you walking
in the shadows
of these trees
sheltering
the backyard playthings
of my daughter:
You pick them up—
they are your daughter's
your son's,
you have a wife
sleeping,
dreaming through
the rest of her life
with you: It is
this love I see
lost in the shadows
of this night, my
mind turning back
with the chill
of late spring.

This is the loss, the love
I bury each night in the shadows,
turning a spadeful of war
over and over, and always,
in the vigilant spin of this earth
digging it up before morning.

GEOGRAPHY LESSON

I have little sense of place
having grown up on the other side
of the world and returned home
to foreigners on foreign soil.
Not once does the family ask questions—
as if I'd gone off for the weekend
to fish or hunt. My place at the table
is the same, same chair, same silverware:
But as I glance up from my meal
I don't recognize the family portrait
hanging on the wall— their faces unfamiliar,
their eyes from another time or country,
another race. Even my grandfather's words,
the words I'd lived by,
dissipate like a ghostly presence
passing through the walls.

                              After dinner
my father stands on the front porch
staring at the lawn I had so often mowed
and played on as a kid:
We share the dark and the silence,
the silence of the world
in response to inarticulate horrors; I flick
a lighted cigarette, watch its red glow
as it traces an arc over the front yard,
land I cannot recognize as home.

CHOPPERS

Always the sound of choppers,
Chinooks, Cobras, Hueys,
a sensual drone of smooth, flashing blades
cutting through air,
churning acrid, Asian heat.

The sound mnemonically beats its way into the night
cutting through darkness like a bayonet
through the top of a C-ration can,
through a block of C-4.

It stays through the spring offensive,
through all the gardening years,
afternoons spent watching the light,
spent listening to the sky.

Years later, women who saw children
killed by the Khmer Rouge, saw heads of children
bashed against trees, became blind
though nothing was wrong with their eyes. And no one
hearing the sound of choppers
fails to look up to search the sky.

Half-deaf from mortar rounds
exploding too close to the bunker,
and artillery firing H&I throughout the night,
ears still pick up the sounds
of rotor blades long before they appear
over trees, above the roof-line.
The heart beats with synchronicity:

Over the paddy a chopper calls out
to the hamlet, *Do not run! Those who run
will be shot as VC.* They run anyway,
stumbling as water sucks at their feet.
It is the line of the rounds as they skip
across the paddy running up their backs—
not the darkening water— that stays,
stays through those afternoons watching the light,
listening to the sky;
it is the water buffalo blinking its eyes
as the wash from the blades drives down dust,
and water rides out in hideous waves
as if the paddy were beaten by rain.

CANOE TRIP

I scouted rapids
from a ridgeline above the river,
its swirling water dark, turbid,
the river banks crumbling, undercut
with this swollen rush from heavy rains.

On my left was a farmer's field,
plowed under, ready for spring planting.
Looking down at the water
I didn't notice the pit
until I was almost at its edge.
It was filled with dead pigs,
a few young ones, the rest mostly fetal
with umbilical cords still attached—
dozens of them heaped over a few large, gray sheep,
a couple of rats, a muskrat
poised, swimming through all that death,
its head resting on the back of a pig.
It looked almost alive swimming there
except its eyes had been plucked by the birds.

I was upwind as I stood at the edge
watching rain pelt down on
small pink bodies heaped several feet high.
Edging back, I skirted around
to the left, walked down along the ridge
on the other side of the pit;
its stench gagged me, and I choked . . .

The dead were on the wire,
sprawled outside the perimeter,
with many more along the tree line;
a few were inside where they'd overrun
a fire team on the left.

In the sun their bodies started
to swell— parts of bodies hung
in the trees, one arm swinging
like a Mexican piñata.

We searched most of the bodies, but the smell
made nearly everyone throw up—
and two were booby trapped.
The week before one had played possum,
and a man was killed next morning
when he came out to search through the dead.

Their stench gagged deep in our lungs,
and defenses were so torn up, engineers
just came and bulldozed all those bodies
together in a pile and buried them
under a few feet of earth—
one arm and part of its hand stuck up,
almost waving good-bye,
before it too was plowed under . . .

I walked back, past the woodchuck
hanging in the tree—
wedged in the V of some branches—
felt the rain
stinging my eyes.

I put in maybe thirty yards downstream
from where I'd landed—
decided to take my chances
with the rocks.

NOTHING TO BE AFRAID OF

A light tropical sleep,
easy, shadowy green as cycad
leaves brushing the air outside your window:
the sun effuses white this early, and the streets—
men in white shirts
moving in and out of traffic
through dazed air outside long ivory windows
holding back the swelling rain

On the street below a small boy chases a lizard
darting in and out of close-covered vegetation

On the hotel roof across the way
some young women
hang out their wash, mostly white,
but a few prints of bright color ruffle
like wings of quetzal and macaw—
two of them see you and wave

In the evening you may have them
for a time that is not theirs;
their bodies will live in you for years
and you will never share
or offer any explanation

You stand there, watching, not waving back,
thinking how easy it is to erase
any trace of a man's life

There is little of the uneasy misgiving,
the turning over in one's sleep
as sharp noises break out shattering
dark perfumed air

The bodies are taken away in the night
as air stealthily closes
over all sound, all movement,
like water closing in over an object
falling against its heavy mass,
settling to the bottom beyond reach
of time, of memory, of fate or heavenly pain

And yet you know the bodies were taken away,
their apartments refurnished and rented by ten,
their names erased like dust in the rain

You look up: first drops splatter, like blood,
on dry streets, the tops of cars,
making the same amorphous, many-tanged star
of plasmic metal falling, cooling,
as it strikes anything flat

White shirts darken as patterns
solidify, tighten, striking the fist of time
driven deep to silence all thought, all
human memory and hate; traffic stalls,
steam rises from hot pavement, the hoods of cars;
air swells, corporeal, incrassate,
a body waking to the rain.

THE SOMME

You kind of wonder every year or so
on hearing of a farmer killed
by plowing up an old artillery shell
somewhere in the fields of France,
the shell working its way up
within reach of the silver tines
and exploding after all these years:
You kind of wonder if they ever change
the numbers in any recorded history of the war
and add one more to the list of the dead.

AFTER THE WAR

On the drive back
from wherever he traveled to,
a flock of birds, possibly wrens,
rose up from the side of the road,
veered across the path of his car,
made a dull *thunk, thunk, thunk*
as bird after bird rolled off the hood,
the windshield . . .

He looked back at soft mounds of feathers
scattered across the pavement,
the sound still in his ears like the sound
a bullet makes when it hits flesh

He never remembered the sound when he was hit,
only the force spinning him back

And he froze, the first time a friend of his
walked up behind him in a bar
and yelled, "Incoming!"

And he didn't hit the ground
when some neighborhood kids threw a cherry bomb
down the street on a warm hazy night last summer

But he remembered that new guy who stepped on a mine—
earth and smoke rising into the air—
remembered the way that man's face drained of all color
waiting for the slick that got there too late.

When he was a kid he buried
a bird he'd killed with his airgun—
the death ritualized, patterned,
instinctual . . .

Body bags, ponchos— the boots sticking out,
aluminum coffins loaded with forklifts

And he didn't slow down,
the birds in his rear view mirror
getting smaller and smaller, sinking into the pavement
stretched far out behind.

CBR
> *for the M17A1 Protective Mask*

At the end of the day,
after all that good training—
first the block of solid
instruction in the bleachers,
the practical demonstrations,
all that practice with the mask:
putting it on, clearing it, testing the seal,
looking like alien creatures
from some Grade B movie in the Fifties,
and then the gas chambers—
first CS, going in masked,
black rubber tight to the face,
flutter valve sucking in and out
with each labored breath, and always
the smell, the taste, of rubber and plastic
swimming in that swirl of smoke,
dark, highly contaminated,
an atmosphere from some other planet
hot and uninhabitable,
then taking it off, reciting for the Sarge
name, rank, serial number—
maybe a question from the twelve standing orders—
and then, with tears streaming down
they're let loose into the fresh, warm
air that clears their eyes and lungs,
brings home the truth that the mask works.

Next, after a short break, the second chamber,
chlorine gas this time,
just like World War I, and they
go in unmasked, double time,
line up inside, against the walls,
two squads at a time, adrenaline pumping,
waiting for the command to mask,
the admonition to clear it
before taking a breath—and one
kid, trying to cheat, had unbuttoned
his canvas bag, and his mask had fallen out,
chlorine turning his brass a sickly green
like his face, his panicking eyes
wild with fright. I looked at him, made him
stand there for a moment and think about it.

Afterwards, when the young recruits
thought the training was over, and they're
standing in formation, given the order
to smoke 'em if they've got 'em,
we'd see what they had learned,
popped four CS grenades
clamped at the ends of mop handles
and ran around the troops, surrounding
the formation with gas,
and some of them stood, put on
their masks as they'd been trained to do,
cleared them, ready for anything
while others ran, dropping equipment
everywhere, rifles, canteens, helmets, pistol belts
and more, and the drill sergeants
were pissed—had to round up
their troops, making them late for dinner.
And this one guy climbed up a tree,
poured water from his canteen

over his head and called for his momma:
and the sergeant yelled, "Get your white
ass out of that tree you dumbfuck
or I'll show you your momma."
And then they'd take all that equipment
dumped on the ground and throw it
in the CS chamber, in a pile, and make all
those dumbfucks go in there and sort it out,
making sure they picked up their own
rifles, and those sergeants would check
the numbers to make sure.

And this one kid just sat there
in the dirt, kneeling, coughing, gas still
thick in the air, and I walked over to him
and held that smoking grenade under his face
and yelled, "Put your mask on," and
he looked up at me, tears running out
of his bloodshot eyes and says, "I've
only got one lung," and I say, "Then
you'd better save that one goddam lung
and put that mask on," and I held
that grenade there, not believing anyone
could be so dumb not to use what he
has learned, knowing that mask would save
all that pain, and yet he wouldn't
put it on and I wouldn't put down that grenade—
And in all my dreams I still stand
there, grenade smoking on the end of that mop handle
holding it close to his face, making him
learn and learn and learn and I'd
still do that today, knowing no matter
how good the training, we never learn anything,
that ignorance brings its own reward,
that I'm still standing there.

ENTROPY

A hand explodes in your face
    You turn aside and drive home

A windshield spiders, webbing across
the low dark ceiling of the night
burning with the deepest blues you've ever seen
    You open the door; a sliver of light
    slices across your cheek, your forehead

A bullet passes through silk without a trace
    You turn a corner in your living room

Somewhere someone is learning—
an artificial arm reaches out, a soft mechanical
purr of its wire tendons gearing down to a touch;
the stainless curved steel of the claw
closes and locks
    The hallway is long, lit by a yellowish light,
    the bulb glowing with a steamy efflorescence
    behind your eyes

Amber, a parrot's blue
color of arm twist, scald,
an eye burned
    You turn to the bath

A face explodes in your hands
the mirror, no eyes,
nothing staring out or back
    Hands tighten and close, cold, white—
    porcelain crumbles with a touch

TO A POET WHO DISDAINS THE THEME OF WAR

Untouched by war
you look out on your land
from the safety of your grand back porch.
You have the freedom of complacency,
the luxury to write of ghostly birds
calling in the evening light,
the last twinges of day
spent nobly remarking
on the way of things.

With a few dollars you can
do anything. Somewhere behind
the shadowed hills, other lives
go on or not—it doesn't matter—
inexorable, the world uncomfortable
and not what you would choose,
and so you don't. Your life
could draw to an inside straight,
and with a poker face you will
rake in the pot, though
such rewards are so beneath you.

My hands are dirty—it was not my choice,
and if I could, perhaps I'd look out on those hills,
jingle the change in my pocket
and feel comfortable, unconcerned
with anything beyond—
my only war the one that raged
with silly thoughts reviewed
inside The New York Times.

Perhaps I too would find the world
so inconsiderate
not to stop upon that ridge,
the blurring line of your horizon,
fading to the nothing that you know so well.

**LEARNING FROM ONE OF MY
LAOTIAN STUDENTS**

"We sat huddled in the corner
of a room with the windows shuttered,
and my grandmother would tell stories;
I was young and only a little frightened—
When I asked about the light
flashing in the distance, the
sound of thunder, a thousand firecrackers
going off almost at once—she
said, smoothing the hair on my forehead,
that the gods were happy and playing in heaven.

"I never learned anything more—
my grandmother died a year
after we came to America, my father
was a general; he never says
anything—I don't even know which side
he was on"—She looks away as if to say
something more, but there is nothing more
in this constant barrage
of half-remembered moments
except, the light, the sound,
buried like a thousand stories
and her heart pounding in that shuttered room.

THE RIGHT THING TO DO:
MISOCZ, UKRAINE, 1942

> *Even the corpse has its own beauty.*
> —Emerson

She was beautiful
And when all the others were told
To strip
At the uneven edge of an ugly cut in the ground,
She pleaded, top button undone, throat open
To the gray wind: others huddled covering the shame
Of a common death, covering bodies unconcerned
With their nakedness, more concerned with gray skies
Blending to black on the horizon, gun barrel black,
Although they couldn't have noticed.

It seemed right not to shoot her
As firing began down at the other end:
Surprisingly, screams were few,
Cries stifled by more than wind.

In war no corpse is beautiful.
At home a natural death,
A death of age, of a body worn out of its soul,
Seems right, evenly just, and what is right
Seems beautiful.

It seemed right not to shoot her
As bodies fell into the gouged eye of earth,
Seemed right to let this one
Who in any other time
Might have been ...
The young man didn't let himself think further—
He told her to go on.

She walked away; her eyes thanked him; there was a prayer
In her eyes as gunfire convulsed the air next to him,
Leaving a high pitched whine, like that of a machine,
Ringing in his ears.

The soldier watched her walk away,
Watched her until all firing was done,
All movement stopped except chains of clouds
Tightening across the sky.

He shot her, aiming for the middle of her back,
Left her where she fell, wind
Whipping hair
Across her beautiful face.

CARNAGE: PROLOGUE

Shot after shot
we pumped through a crevice
at the coiled snake
holed up in piles
of discarded rocks

Fired again and again
at green and gold stripes
wound tight around
black flesh
flinching with each shot

Then, our fusillade ended,
we pushed those rocks aside, and with a stick
the limp, shattered flesh
was lifted ceremoniously
onto a low crusty branch

We stood still, surrounding our sacrifice
streaked with viscera strung along the stripes—
it hung there, BBs interrupting
its scaly patterns, branches quivering
with the weight.

TAKING THE EASY WAY

A friend of mine
shot himself in the foot,
carefully aimed not to shatter
a bone: said he was just
cleaning his .22 before going into
the Air Force; all it did was delay
his time by three weeks—hardly worth it.

Another guy, actually the friend of a friend
in San Francisco, at the Art Institute,
got drunk, popped some pills,
bent his arm backwards on a table
and had someone jump on his elbow, breaking it
the wrong way; splinters of bone
jutted out of his flesh, and his face
just as white as his bone—

Jesus, all that just to avoid the draft;
and with a mind like that
he would have done just fine in Vietnam.

II.

Preguntaréis: Y donde estan las lilas?
Y la metafisica cubierta de amapolas?
Y la lluvia que a menudo golpeaba
sus palabras llenandolas
de agujeros y pajaros?

venid a ver
la sangre por las calles,
venid a ver la sangre
por las calles!

—Pablo Neruda, "Explico Algunas Cosas"

**NIGHT TACTICS: TRAINING EXERCISE
WITH WATER MOCCASIN**

We chased it through parting grass
down a rough slope, over
rock and Georgia clay.
Sarge got there first,
struck it with a walking stick
he'd notched with every kill;
it turned, opening its cold gray mouth
and took a butt stroke to the head:
dead it twitched and raw blood ran
the blackness of its length.

We hung it by the bleachers,
next to where I taught night tactics in the day—
laid out the rules for
covering fields of fire, using a garrotte,
moving noiselessly through grass and swamp,
knowing what it takes to stay alive.

SEARCH AND DESTROY

They came out of the hootch
with their hands up—surrendered—
and we found all that rice
and a couple of weapons. They
were tagged and it all seemed so easy—
too easy, and someone started to torch
the hootch and I stopped him—something
was funny. We checked the hootch
a couple times more; I had them probe it
like we were searching for mines and
a lucky poke with a knife
got us the entrance to a tunnel.
We didn't wait for any damn
tunnel rats—we threw down
CS and smoke and maybe two hundred
yards to our right two gooks popped up
and we got 'em running across the field,
nailed 'em before they hit the trees.
We went to the other hole and popped more
gas and smoke and a fragmentation grenade
and three gooks came out coughing, tears
and red smoke pouring out of their eyes and
nose. We thought there were more
so we threw in another grenade and one of the
dinks brought down his arms, maybe he started
to sneeze with all that crap running out of his face,
maybe he had a weapon concealed, I didn't know,
so I greased him. Wasn't much else I could do.
A sudden move like that.

WINNING HEARTS AND MINDS

She clasps the child to her breast—
cries as her hootch burns. Her husband
fought back—lies there—upper butt stroke
so hard it broke the phenolic stock: vengeance—
a futile gesture—spitting betel juice
into the wind.

She has lost one son to the VC, another
to an air strike: She remembers the soft rain
of dirt falling out of the sky—
sees his chest opened like a fruit,
dug open with the nails and pulled apart—
his organs glistened like a melon.

She sobs; her eyes sing hate; her child,
clutched tighter, cries above the flames.

A marine screams, "Shut the fuck up!"

A scrawny pig is shot and tossed on the flames;
rice burns, pops like a flare.

She runs, tit flapping against her chest,
falls
against the hard luck of Vietnam.

INTERROGATION

A man sits in the afternoon,
crosslegged, arms tied behind to a stake;
the major is angry; that man knows, lies
about what he knows, plays dumb. The major
knows little of the language; his interpreter is bored.
The man is wasting the major's time;
there are lives at stake; there will be other prisoners,
other afternoons. "You VC!" "No! No VC!"
The major is impatient; he pulls out his knife,
plunges it into the thigh near the
prisoner's groin and rips down
to his knee. "You VC!" The major walks away.

BIEN HOA, 1968

We were talking in this bar
after the fight broke up: music,
the bar girls, the heat—it was
easy to set someone off; it was
like everyone was primed, a charge, a claymore
that could be set off by static.
Anyway, he said this was something,
ordered another round; "I love this place,"
he said, "just extended—again." He said
for three years before Nam he'd had
training companies; it was "Police
the company area, sergeant," or
"Make sure the troops have the right
pair of boots on" (the ones with the dots
or the ones without), or "Paint the
day-room, sarge," or "Line 'em up
for some shots," or "Give 'em a
surprise inspection." He'd make them see
the training film twice, just so they got it.
Once he spent two weeks dealing with all
the flak over an NCO who'd hassled
one of the trainee's wives; she'd complained to
the battalion commander. Anyway, no more
training; "Isn't this great?" he said—
the dancer flashed a shot of her pelt. I said, "Yeah"
and went to the john. I pissed the last two beers
and a hand grabbed my cock, asked if I wanted some
help—I said, "No thanks, maybe next time, but
I'll buy you a drink." She was cute and her
hand felt good. I went back to the bar, ordered
the Major a drink, and the chick, and myself.
He yelled, "Isn't this great!"—again. She put her arms
around his waist, shouted something in his ear
over the music. I didn't think anything at the time.
He shouted, as the girl pushed her tongue in his ear,
"I love this fucking war; if it wasn't
for this fucking war, I'd go crazy."

NIGHT AMBUSH

Last man through the gate
turn out the lights—MP humor
fuck 'em—no moon, starlight and shadow
only the sound of the packs rubbing, shuffling
with each step—a few metal clinks—
Get that equipment squared away—a whisper
passed down from the front—pass it on—
counting shadows, keep your distance, a hiss,
peeved off, fuck this shit—ammo, canteen click,
the sound of breathing through the mouth—
the pig heavy, catching on the brush,
reflective tape bobbing, disappearing, lost for
too long a time—interval screwed up? the
dumbshit taken out? He's there, don't do it again—
loud noise, dry twigs, sound of moving through the brush—
they can hear this in Hanoi—halt—hey, hold it up—
two years in the Army and they can't keep an interval—
move back—bunched up one homemade claymore could
take out the lot—second squad drops off, sets up,
puts out claymores, checks overlapping fire, lays out a flare,
straightens the pin on a grenade—magazines
piled to the front—eases back, waits, checks in—
first squad off to the left, 100 m. away, good block if they
come parallel to the trail—animal movement, brush rustle,
eyes stare at the sound, see things that aren't
there, look away, stare too long and anything's
out there—a twitch, too quiet, almost dozing—
snapping back, barrel cold to the touch—press
a mag to the forehead, keep awake, long legs,
the best smile, can feel her breasts pressed against
my chest—the warmth of a bath together, scrubbing her back
as she leans forward stretching her legs against the tub—
drifting off—sound of water running, warming the bath,
voices, movement, a claymore rakes the approach,
rock n' roll two mags, a few rounds through the leaves

overhead crack into the trees—nothing but
gunpowder smell, smoke, muzzle flash
still in the eyes—wait, no movement, no sound,
check it out or wait? wait, wait until light—
call it in, 2 clicks, call sign, a whisper
and wait—sound of blood rushing
through the brain, white flash if the eyes close—
a dry sweat, something crawling on the face—
brush it away—push back the steel pot, press
the cold metal of another magazine to forehead and wrists,
wait, doze, look up at the stars, a few shining through the leaves
disappear in gray light—two dead and no one came back
to take 'em out—bodies riddled with shot—
a good night, hot chow waiting, move out before the sun.

STANDARD

A bleached skull
wired to an APC
mocking it all
with its separate
teeth
spins on its track
churning roostertails
of red dirt
and grins
white and hard
at Charlie

GB

> *And behold joy and gladness, slaying*
> *oxen, and killing sheep ...*
> —Is 23.13

For every class the sheep is roped and walked
to the familiarly worn patch of ground before the stands
where young men training in chemical weapons
sit talking, smoking, waiting for the break to end,
the practical demonstration to begin.

The sheep, tethered, nibbles a single blade of grass
as the break ends and the Captain explains, *A single drop ...*
tightness in the chest ... muscles rigid ... pupils
pinpointed... . Carefully, slowly, he places a drop
on the leathery tip of the sheep's nose, black, glistening.

Nothing, nothing for seconds and seconds until the wise,
calm look on his face changes instantly
and a single convulsion throws him on his back,
his heavy wool caking with dust as his legs stiffen and lock;
his ears shake like a torn piece of flesh dangling
from a wolf's mouth, and his head chatters against the dirt.

Inside, it is dark, consciously dark, like the starless
nights where shapes moved black against black, circling—
worse than his worst dreams of lynx, worse than
a grizzly sow ripping from the inside out—
lungs turned to stone, flesh like a plaster cast,
bones calcified, chipping, disintegrating, in movement
sharp as the arc of a sacrificial knife.

He waits for the sting of the atropine,
sharp plunge of the needle as an auto-injector
is jammed into his side; always
it was the bringing back that amazed him,
how he could feel death's teeth grazing his throat,
and then, so simply, look up into the sun, jump
onto his feet and run to a warm patch of luxuriant grass,
but this time cold blades of teeth
cut in to the core and all sensation, all
thought and dreams turned to black ice.

His eyes froze, and his solid, swollen tongue,
as he lay under the passing clouds,
the stares of men in their black masks,
the Captain's heavy breath as he pounded the sheep's heart.
The Captain, unused to failure,
has little to say; he mutters that
it always worked before, says he'd try it again
if he had another sheep. He steps back,
gives a final look at the corpse,
and walks away.

The men pull off their masks, fold them in their canvas bags;
they walk out of the bleachers, take long puffs on cigarettes,
smoke spinning under the circling circles of the sun.
Dazed as though having lost too much blood,
dreaming of sex, contending, a whimsical parry
with forces of uncontrolled will, they spill over
into the trees, stand in the shade, watch two privates
dressed in unstarched fatigues, ignominious, unhurried,
bundle the bone-hard sheep into the back of a deuce-and-a-half.

Far off, in Utah, the sky opens, deepens, over sheep running
from hill to hill—from a vantage point high enough
they look like white flowers moving in the wind,
moving in the candent haze of light
offering by fire, without blemish, the sacrifice,
the lesson, of sheep.

THE SIAMESE SYPH

On R&R in Bangkok you
banged away day after day,
night after night, and when
you were sore, had had enough
for a year, you walked out into
the light, smelled the green water
in the klong and felt the heat
ache in your gut—your cock
so sore you thought you'd
caught the Asian clap;
so you showered, used Comet cleanser
to wash off your balls—and they swelled,
swelled up to the size of grapefruit,
and you never got V.D.

BEGGING

A child beggar
stops you in the street,
a fresh red flower in her hair;
her mother waits, watching in the background,
scarlet betel juice
filling her mouth like blood

You rush on never meeting her eyes,
embarrassed by the truth of this common encounter—
the truth pulling at your sleeve

At night your dreams have the same eyes;
you shake the shoulders of this child,
this life, even your own,
shake hell out of its soul

No face ever again appearing
in the mirrors,
the reflective mirages
catching your downward stare—
red flowers endlessly falling
at your feet

You turn in the black heat,
a small hand twisting the material
of your life

You catch hold
tearing into the crowd,
pushing past eyeless gods
and faces crumbling into the street

You run through the market place—
the head of a goat in a silver dish
stares back at you; from every corner and arch
eyes lift from the stone

Canvas canopies rip and tear in the sun,
noise deafens and numbs;
you are pulled through the moving crowd
by something you still believe to be true:
you grab hold of your own begging,
a small hand catching in the slow blade of a fan
bent and rasping like truth against the wire guard
begging to stop, begging to forgive

ROLLING THUNDER

Utapao, a sunny bright afternoon,
warm sky cloudless, almost white beneath
the strike of Asian light. Camouflaged B-52's—
their underbellies the color of sky—take off
in wave after wave, black smoke trailing,
nacelles shimmering like a desert mirage.
Outside the base, curious, dispassionate Thais watch,
their fingers hooked in the chain-link fence
topped with barbed wire strands. You wonder
what they think and see as the huge machines
scream off on their afternoon runs, regular as
soap operas on American T.V.—war as far removed
as *Bonanza* or *Lost In Space*, their characters—
Hoss, the Robot—speaking in Thai as you watch in a bar
at the Officers' Club, and you want to go
to Chiang Mai to watch elephants haul in the teak,
to live in the hills—offer at a Buddhist shrine
flowers and incense, a candle guttering
into the rest of your life.

ON THE GULF OF SIAM

There is a passion in this stillness
Trees with blossoms orange as monk's cloth
Shelter merchants resting
Before returning to the sun
Selling bathers Pepsi and bananas
Red fish braised on sticks and love
A sheltered cove cradles rocks
Strewn on the shore like the ruins
Of an ancient temple the serenity
Of stone statuary shattered
Broken by the furious caprice of the sea
She darkens the stain of old moss
Clinging to rocks
And with warm hands
Eases the bodies of lovers dreaming
Of the effortless movement slowly flowing
Flowing out and out beyond reach
Of the moon they dream of being drawn
Slowly into the sun of never returning
To a land much loved by war

DUST-OFF

You watch the dust-off power in
taking a dozen rounds in the tail
and all the wounded are put
on board except one guy whose guts
are all over the ground, sliding
over the red, dusty earth,
and no one wants to touch him,
his organs quivering and bright,
but another round spat through
the cockpit spidering the glass,
and the pilot screams, *Let's move!*
as you run over scooping the
guts in your hands, piling them back
in the abdomen, the cavity filling with blood,
and then he's lifted, everyone careful not
to tip him on his side, on board the
chopper and he gets off, lifting into the
sky that opens into white—and you
remember the way the dead back home
are covered with a sheet that white,
what it felt like to see the sky come down, white,
muslin sucked into nose and mouth
with the last breath, feeling the white on your
eyes as you look up, see the sky turn green,
smelling, tasting, of plastic.

BRINGING IT IN

Assault dive
sharp, steep angle
C-130 loaded with mines

Clouds separate,
open to Chicom tracers
green as Christmas

PSP strip, mortared
covered with sprays of red
dust—flap malfunction,
the landing rough and quick

Unload, forms signed—
a few pleasantries before
take off—leaving behind
red cratered earth,
pools filling with rain,

The black char skeleton
of a tree, a body
outside the wire.

HUMPIN' THROUGH THE BOONIES

Get down—a sniper's rd ricochets to the right,
where? anyone got it? off to the left, the
tree line, eleven o'clock, no, to the front,
rake the tree line, nothing, let's go,
spread out, keep your distance—
more harassment than anything, getting
down in the dirt, sucking dust all afternoon—
another rd, another hundred yards, heavy pack,
hot helmet, sweat pouring into the eyes,
and they watch, unaffected by everything,
dry dirt caking the sweat—fuck the army,
FTA on the helmet ahead of me, check out
the hedgerow—so thick a bangalore
wouldn't make a dent—stay away from the gate,
wring out the sweat, watch for tripwires, a spider's
thread in the sun, canteen half full, warm, not
worth the effort—another rd, 2, 3, AK by the sound
keep moving, keep awake up there, hold it, hold it!,
movement, sleight of hand, what's up? get to the
hamlet late afternoon, don't take no shit, not today,
too many days (exactly) like this, hey! pump a 79 rd
over there 150 m, edge of the dike, to the right
20 m—another rd zings in, the flash, the explosion—
wait, get up, nothing, they're gone, nobody's there
except old women, kids, a few dogs
fuck this shit, zippo diplomacy, they were here dammit
can smell it, all that rice for the women, bullshit,
nothing, again nothing, check that hootch,
do it right this time, ain't no damn social call,
no shit?, burn it, two klicks and we're there,
not the easy way, dumbshit, through the paddy—
call it in, ETA LZ Red, 17:15, move it out,
hear them damn birds, let's go, second squad
mount up, the rotor wash cool, too tired
even to sweat, anyway.

WHY I DIDN'T PUT IN MY TWENTY

After moving through wet jungle
all afternoon
I felt something strange between my legs
and dropped my pants.
A leech was hanging onto one of my testicles
sucking all the blood out of my balls.
I looked at it, observed the way it curled
up in the fetal position when I grabbed
hold of its tail, and I thought, dispassionately,
how strange the world is,
how strange that God created leeches,
that man created the Army
for leeches to feed on.

COMMENDATION

A chill of rain
and this hot sun

layers of mist rising
twisting in crazed arcs
as a man passes through

It is the restraint
of distance
looking out
mountains, like targets, no nearer
than before——their green
so deep a man could drown

Movement
and nothing, not even the war,
comes close

Strange
to have gone this far
and not
worth it.

MOVING THE MINES FROM SATTAHIP TO NAKHON PHANOM

for John Baky

"Don't ever get a jeep
between two deuce-and-a-half's
when you put a convoy together,"
directed the Transportation Officer
as he continued his briefing:
"Just last week a lieutenant wanted to move up
the convoy, had his driver pull out to pass,
and sure enough another vehicle
came down the road, a Mercedes, a big truck
brightly painted with murals of the afterlife,
careening from side to side, kicking up dust,
going full tilt like a VC truck driver
hauling ass down the Ho Chi Minh trail,
and the jeep pulled in between two trucks
in the convoy, and in a typical chain reaction
everyone decelerated, except this one driver
who was too close to the jeep,
and the jeep hit from behind struck the rear
of the truck ahead, and the truck behind
hit the jeep again, its large beam of a
bumper going up over the back of the jeep,
over that lieutenant's head, and the truck
slammed to a stop, but the jeep kept going,
and the lieutenant's head got ripped off—
here, I've got pictures"—
They're in black and white, blood the color
of OD, just a shade darker, and the head—
like John the Baptist's—that's all I can
think of, a picture in my Bible
in confirmation class, its head detached
like distant memories of war,
like luck that has just run out
like blood.

INTELLIGENCE

The body was lying there in the open,
stretched out along a hedgerow
intersecting a dike—
unusual since they went to great lengths
to remove all their dead.

I thought it a trick—an easy ambush
as the platoon was bunched up
waiting for the body to be searched—
I had everyone spread out, take cover,
and search the wood line that formed
a broad L to our front.

But we weren't really that close for an
effective ambush—unless the area
was targeted by mortars,
so I thought it booby-trapped and told
everyone to back off, to get behind the dike—

I had two guys put a noose around
the neck of the corpse and fall back.
I told everyone to get down and then
gave the order to pull—

Both men were squatting behind the dike
and they yanked—hard—and fell back,
tumbling over each other as the head pulled off
and everyone laughed—the rest of the body barely moved
it had been laying there too long—

Even my old experienced E-6,
who never cracked a smile, laughed
at the two yahoos grinning, falling over each other.
"Shit for brains, you two could fuck up a wet dream,"
and we laughed; the head rolled and looked up at the sky.

We emptied a magazine into the corpse;
I thought that would set off any
pressure-release type device,
and then it was searched—nothing—
no orders, no maps, nothing—not even
a picture of his wife or his kids.

SAIGON, 1969

Almost run over by a Honda
while crossing the street,
I mutter some obscenity
under my breath—
the street crowded, the black market
flooded with merchandise
ripped off from the PX
the night before

A woman comes out of a shop,
walks along beside me and says something
I don't understand:
she puts her hand over
my crotch—I say no and walk on—
she squeezes, says Number 1. I say,
yes, number 1, but no thanks—
and she stops, says something obscene
I can't comprehend, but the high
pitch of her voice rings in my ears—
You number 10 GI, she screams, her
voice exploding in a language that any
dumb American can understand.

NOT GETTING IT RIGHT

I

A dumbness thickens behind you
And air, like rain forest footprints,
Compresses and waits: you stand at the locked gate
Staring at the garden, its stone path
Lined with flowers more fragrant from the rain;
The taxi turns around and parks,
Its engine still running. You hear
The bell ring, and after a time, as you're ready
To press it again, you notice movement
Behind an unlit, translucent screen. A woman
Walks out with a lantern held up to her face:
You speak with a few words of Vietnamese
And she responds, breaking into English that tells you
The woman you are seeking has moved; she
Doesn't know where, and you couldn't
Quite catch how long ago she left. You
Thank her as she turns to go in, lantern light
Following her, arcing over and back,
Across wet and reflective stones.

II

Later, that night, you return to your room,
Watch gecko lizards climb the wall
Next to your bed; you wonder where she had gone,
Learning the world just doesn't wait
During its inexorable change. You are impatient;
The odor of an Asian flower in a carafe of water
Next to your bed reminds you of her, close,
In your arms, in this very bed—the scent
Dissipates in stale air. You return to your loss;
Your sweat soaks into your sheets
As you lie smoking, thinking, dreaming of what
You have lost, what loss you will live for,
And return to as life explodes in the street
Below your room, calling you home.

BIOGENESIS

On the windowsill
The broken stem of a philodendron
Refracts in a half-filled
Glass of water, new shoots
Turning the water gray in the light
Another prayer
Another reparation

And Belief strong as a god
Strikes the tails from lizards
The arms from starfish
Cuts platyhelminthes into tiny pieces

From every piece—
    red dye smoke pours
    from nose and eyes and mouth
A new life
    a woman times her tricks
    with a cigarette
A new prayer
    both hands fit easily around a mortar round
    as it slowly slides down the smooth hot tube
From every wound—
    the cells contract, like a bargirl
    contortionist, in the antiseptic phase
A new belief
    self-immolation: a piece of the monk's
    orange robe—the edges, charred black,
    fall off with a touch of the hand
A new beginning
    a claymore clears a path

And does it hurt, my friends
To know part of yourself
Goes in every direction
Away from your home?

Will you grow another leg
From that charred stump?
Will your mind grow back
With no trace of the napalm blisters?

If I take your hand
And bury it in the earth burned breathless
Will another child grow
With eyes so dark and cool
No fires will ever grow there?

WORDS

You needn't have said anything lying there,
knowing your words as I did;
I knew each choking sound that raged
against your shattered throat.

Then, when your face was still,
words still flowing from your lips,
I knew that you were home again
making love under a gentler sky.

Off in the trees wistful traces of smoke
lift like dreams from the smoldering earth:
This is no country for young men,
the dead in one another's arms.

ONCE AGAIN

She raises the lantern
to your questioning face

Reads your eyes
as your words stumble in the dark

You learn the truth
of the nothing she can tell

She bows politely as you thank her
and turns in the bobbing light

The garden turns bronze
in amber reflections of a half-crazed moon

The frog pond is silent
and you watch as she slips past the trees

The room empties of any delight—
screened walls turn in, pivot

In the timbre of shadows pleasuring off
to some other place

A yellow carp rises and descends
without taking the still fly

Your mind follows the ball of light
wading in and out of the trees

PATAYA BEACH R&R, 1968

A monkey leaps from shoulder to
shoulder, looking for food—
it stays chained to a tree all day
as hotel guests pose for the camera,
both guests and monkey grinning:

Years later the photo fades
as if overexposed in the bright light
of Asia, heat and light a blur
as if the camera had moved.

My face fades in the light
of history, the laugh of that monkey,
war exploding in the background
behind those flowering trees.

LESSONS LEARNED

It seems like every week
another pamphlet was placed inside my box
waiting to be read and initialed
before routing to the next L.T.
Every week another lesson learned in Vietnam.
Booby traps, weapons systems, new
enemy tactics, all noted and registered,
all part of the training.

Over a beer in the Officers' Club,
conversation turned to the last
lesson learned, of a friend who'd
missed the slender thread linking
a 105 round to a pressure-release type
device, and triggered the damn thing
with one wrong step—the way
you'd miss a few yards of
monofilament that tangled in your boot
hiking a trail around a lake last summer.

All these years, lessons learned and
unlearned, this one still stays,
this lesson of one false step,
the wrong move that's always made
no matter the training, no matter
how much care is taken:

Somewhere, a spider's web
catches in the sun
on this move from one pattern of light
to the next.

We walk on carefully placing each step
slowly on the firm ground beneath
almost catching something
out of the corner of an eye:
The earth moves under foot,
and the sky is still on fire.

III.

Keep moving, friend, and don't look down.

—John Balaban, *After Our War*

CONVERSATION

He says, "You've never seen anything
unless you've seen a man hit in the chest
with an RPG round."

I said, "I guess not," and drank on
into the heavy Asian night, weighted and packed.

I thought how many times you could say,
"You've never seen anything unless you've
seen ..." and then go on, just fill in
the blanks ...

    an F-4 Phantom drop napalm along a tree line

    an illumination round light up the perimeter
    as night probes catch in the outer defenses

    body bags lined up at the edge of the pad,
    rotors rippling the plastic as they descend

And I said, long after that night, after I'd felt their
names carved in that stone, "You've never seen anything ...
anything ... anything ..."

BACK IN THE WORLD

It was weird coming back—
everyone cheered when the plane
touched down at Frisco—tires
screeched on the runway and the whole
plane just about lifted up again
with all that noise. I didn't
feel anything—I'd left as much or more
behind as I'd come home to.
I went back to school on the GI bill—
chickenshit one-sixty a month. It took a month's
pay just to buy the books. But I didn't
go right away, I tried to but I couldn't,
I registered late, just couldn't go through
all that rinky-dink hassle and I sat out
a term—stayed in my room for four months
and didn't talk to anybody. I couldn't
face those damn kids. I didn't get
unemployment either—I couldn't deal
with that though I was entitled. I would now,
but then I thought I could take care of myself—
I'd been there—I didn't need any help—didn't
want no damn chickenshit civilians fucking
me over, making me wait in line
another damn time. After awhile
I had to go out and talk—to hear my voice again—
I'd talk to anyone just so I knew
I could do it again—the guy
who fixed my car, I talked to him
for hours—he was in World War II
and I wasted a couple afternoons with him.
When I went back to school the first day
they'd fucked up—given me the wrong
classroom number and time for this course I'd
signed up for. So I missed the first
class. I went to see this prof. and tell

him what happened. He had this lecture
see, all typed up, would let me have it
to make a copy of, but he had to be sure
I'd return it right away. He said, "You'll
bring it back, for sure, this afternoon? It's
my only copy, so you'll bring it back, right?"
I said, "Yeah," but I was thinking about having my stripes,
being a squad leader, responsible for
my men, their lives, and megabucks worth of equipment and
such, and here he kept asking me if I'd bring
that chickenshit paper back to him. "You'll
bring it back, right; you won't run off with it
and forget, right?" "Yeah, right." I knew then
I'd never make it.

WHAT THERE IS

'57 Chevy
channelled and chopped,
a woman with more than
anyone could handle,
religion, falconry,
football, and a hundred
other passions and nothing
is ever the same

Gone back to
the car misses and spits,
its pedal pushed to the floor,
ball game turned off at the half,
peregrine flown from the leather wrist,
and the woman nothing special, not anyone
you'd care to talk to

About the only thing that matters,
caught back of the eye,
downed like a chopper
slammed into the side of a hill,
burning orange into the trees,
is this strange recollection—
true or not—seeing death
as a man you beat at cards,
as your childhood, as history,
as part of the landscape,
as beauty
terrible and fulfilling

BACK IN THE LAND OF THE BIG PX

Once, when I was sick,
I woke up sweating, my sheets wet
at noon, in August, in Philadelphia—
the air in my apartment stale,
the air outside rank
with the smell of a stale city in summer.

A fish hawker passed by
crying out with some old world charm.

I looked out into the street, saw two cops
pick up their weekly stash—
small bills and some coke
from the dudes who sold dope every Thursday
from noon until three.

I went to the back window
and looked out over the black tar roof
of the second floor apartment below me
and threw out some bread for the birds—

A dozen pigeons came within minutes,
their snotty beaks pecking at crusts,
their pink feet scrabbling over oily tar
softening in city heat. I picked up a sling

Shot I'd made and placed a stove bolt
in its leather pouch;
I pulled back aiming for the broad
back of a pigeon pecking away only a few feet
below. The bolt skimmed off his back
and embedded in tar.

They all rose a few feet off the roof and settled
back as if nothing, not even their lives,
were more important than those few
moldy slices of bread.

I picked up a wood screw, fired a direct hit
this time in the middle of its back,
but it bounced off and again they flew away,
only to return with their ravenous disregard,
their intense hunger compelling me
to prey on that hunger, that blind
drive slapping the hard face of reason.

I found another projectile—a nail this time—
and aimed at that pigeon so damned unfazed
by the hit that he took. I pulled back
as far as I could and released.

The nail sliced through his feathers
and stuck into his back as he lifted
above the roof. I watched him circle
over rowhouses across the alley,
backyards filled with trash,
a dead cat swelling in the sun.

I threw out more bread, and they all came
back, including the one I'd stuck with that nail;
but the nail had worked out, and he ate as if nothing
had happened.

I laughed through the sweat, the smell of hot tar,
and I wished
I had never come home.

A MATTER OF FACT: NICARAGUA, 1983

Rain forest mist
a heavy green grayed by distance,
haze palling the sound

Disguised as game trail,
this narrow path beneath treads soft—
layers of spongy leaves,
dark branches, muted chatter
up above

And this new road
carved like a knife's scar
runs deep
not paved, debris piled
along the way, brush
clogging the half-filled ditch

There is no pain, no smell
of corpses reeking
in the sodden air

There is the dream of flowers
perfumed, heavy, poisoned
as the scent digs deep
into the lungs

An old bus painted
with bright unearthly colors
spews out soft earth,
red, gouged,
in some omniscient view
like the face warned,
cautioned against
any resistance—
You are ours, he said
to do with as we please.

The bus, its visionary palette,
swerves and sways—
colors of an afterlife
downshifting for an inclined curve—
a halting shudder
as gears grind and the wheels
spin

There is no thought of death
as carbines breathe fire,
as red flowers drip poison
on darkened earth
still heavy with the rain

There is the body thrown clear,
six others bleeding in their seats,
blood sticky on the feet
of those who found them hours later,
took them to a church and lined them
out, in the shadows of that church,
where they were stripped and bathed,
soft hands washing crimson
smears from breast and throat,
bodies still supple,
caressed as if by lovers
as the blood runs clear

If there is mourning
no one thinks it so;
it is a commonplace
among the woodsmoke,
heavy flowers, new roads,
and the rain that comes
that afternoon, clearing the haze,
helping to wash
the bodies clean.

BOUNDARY WATERS

I can walk down a trail now—
an old portáge—
and not check out the branches
I push away from my face:
I still look down at the ground
and sometimes find myself stopping
to probe a well-placed pile of leaves,
an old log rotting and wet.
I notice the signs, shift
the weight of my pack.
Looking up to the sun
I bring myself back,
saying out loud to myself,
*I doubt if the damned Potawatami
ever booby-trapped deer shit or bear*,
and flick the stool over
with a stick, and laugh, and walk on.

Once, a year or two ago, through
kermi and rempi, I slipped, sunk
down in a natural hole, and I screamed
dreaming of punji stakes covered with feces
cutting into my ankle and calf.
I laughed, not even a sprain. But every
deer within miles lay down for the day.

It was like the week before deer season—
I'd see a dozen every morning and then nothing
on opening day.

But I'd be crazy to go out there then,
gunfire from every direction,
shooting at everything that moves,
better to wait—I have a crossbow—
accurate, easily concealed, and I can carry
a small deer for miles.

Before the shot
I ask for my breath to steady,
my eye to sight true,
my arrow to cut deep to the heart.
I thank the animal
for what he gives me,
for what I have learned.

There is so much wind today
the birds have not come out to feed.
I've watched blue jays, grackles, starlings
cut through snow—
the flakes heavy, shaken off their backs,
their wings, with a ruffle, almost a shiver
of cold—the way you'd feel in a Chinook
coming out of the heat to 3,000 feet,
or the sweat that chilled the back—
bracketed by mortars with so little cover,
no fall back defense.

Once, in elephant grass, rounds no more
than a foot overhead, we hit the ground hard
and fired, just inches above the hot, red earth—
and got a few, and they broke off:
an old E-6 who'd been through Korea
told us we'd have to *make like a snake*—
an old joke, but it worked.

Last spring I saw faces, camouflage,
the point of a recon team. The leaves
played tricks, the light, the time of year—
even the smell of earth and air brought it back.
I got down low, slid back, looked
for the logical ambush
along that avenue of approach. But it was
only the leaves, the thinking.

I don't see that now. I canoe
straight to the islands, set up camp,
lie awake listening to the stars,
the trees, the lake—sometimes a beaver
slaps his tail on the smooth water
when it's dark and I'm lying there
restless, unable to sleep—
the sound of a mortar round
hitting a half-drained paddy
on the other side of the world—
I turn over and it's almost easy to sleep.

CONFIRMED

After confirmation
the minister came over to his house
to join in celebration: all his relations—
a dozen uncles and cousins—were there,
and as a joke the reverend put on
the young man's red blazer,
sleeves six inches too short, no possible way
to button that one gold button in the front,
but everyone laughed; the minister was good at that,
making everyone feel good about himself and God.

Growing up it was hard to please
any adult: teacher, father, minister,
or in basic his platoon sergeant
who always found a wrinkle in his bunk,
a trace of Brasso hidden inside his belt buckle
or under insignia pinned to his collar—
for this he must have got a hundred gigs.
Even scoring 470 on the PCPT wasn't enough
to get that man to let up just one bit,
his ass so tight he could have bent
the barrel of an M-14 rammed up his butt.

And after the war where no one was pleased
with anything anyone ever did,
it was just the same—
wife, child, employer after employer
until no one had any expectations left,
and if anyone were ever pleased
it was just by accident
the way he missed that curve
on County Highway G and hit a tree
going seventy ... or eighty.

"A BEAUTIFUL DAY FOR BOMBING"

—Air Force Weathercaster
in Saudi Arabia, 11 Feb. 91

Bombs lifted into place
complete the aesthetic
planes naked without them—
wings hold their bombs like children

F-15E's taxi along the apron, long
impatient lines, waiting to catch their dream of the sky:
over Basra, target sighted and held
in the cross hairs, bombs tip forward,
spin slowly toward bridges, buildings,
communication networks, waterworks, refineries—
at their release, antiaircraft spinning up, the plane pulls
back and away, cuts in its afterburner and shoots
quickly out of range, all day, a beautiful day for bombing,
and into the night: against neon-black sky,
before targets explode into flame, its afterburner
glows like the sun, cuts out, disappears
as the plane returns to Dhahran.

Eidetic imagery, tracers, bomb-glow, antiaircraft,
afterburners leaving tracks across the sky,
like cloud chambers in science class,
particles unseen, but their skewed imprints cut through
heavy smoke, thick vapor, that parts easily, quickly,
like skin under a surgeon's knife.

In Ninevah, near a mosque
sculpted white and smooth as bone,
a minaret serves as an aiming stick
and a surgical strike turns up antiquities
archaeologists would never have found,
except by accidental stumbling
over the Testament of Mesopotamian brick

In a hospital, without anesthetic, a surgeon
removes the leg of a young girl, above the knee,
folds a flap of skin over the bone, puts on a bandage
wrapped into a white bundle, swaddled and taped,
the way that girl wrapped her first doll
in a bright bundle of cloth

And bundles of fire rain down from B-52's
based in Diego Garcia, bombs cradled
in their bays like sleeping children

And out of this—
Irony, our one human contribution—
the bombs rain down, the blood
rains up, as though earth
were sky, the world, its physical laws, turned upside down:
irony of ironies—smart bombs in a dumb world
and our only intelligence can't even tell us
how many are the dead

NOTHING PERSONAL

I

At 3 A.M. Ernest heard his door break in
shattering the 1X4 molding, his keep-the-honest-
people-honest lock, and the screen bent in
from too many hands pushing on it over the years.

Mother of God, swore Ernest reaching for the light.

A truck driver wearing a sweat-stained cowboy hat
pushed back on his head, a concho belt, buckle
bigger than his fist, stood there, grinning,
holding a tire iron long as a baseball bat,
mewling something about kicking somebody's ass;
stood there, smacking the flat end of the iron
across his palm, looking around for someone
to beat the shit out of.

Ernest could hear the whine of a diesel
parked on the highway, knowing, as he'd said before
that he should never have built that close to the road.
Get the hell out of here, spoke Ernest less loudly
than he'd intended.

The trucker laughed a giggly sort of high-on-drugs
laugh and smashed a rack of dishes.

Ernie backed up, tripped, scrambled for his shotgun
standing against the far corner of the room.
Get the hell out before you get hurt!

That grizzly-chested trucker hauled back, whipped
his iron bar across the room. Ernie ducked. The steel
bounced off the chewed up wall, fell
at the trucker's feet. *Dammit man, get out!*

Picking up the iron, grunting as he bent over
his heavy Coors gut, the trucker straightened up
drawing that iron bar back behind his head.
No chances left, Ernie blew his lungs out,
left them embedded in the wall.

The iron dropped: like a wounded bear
the driver stumbled to his truck, climbed up
into the cab, slumped over the wheel to die.

II

In Vietnam, in Quang Ngai province, at fire base
Rita, a VC company overran the phoo-gas,
the claymores, the concertina, and a young soldier
fired half a clip at an opiate crazed
VC who kept running, even as another
6, 7, 8 rounds spun through his chest,
and still he kept running, his weapon firing
as he spun to the half-dead earth, and John Henry Johnson
caught one of those rounds in his thigh
and screamed, not so much for being hit,
as for being hit by a dead man.

III

Flashback, déjà vu, coincidence culled
from the sum of mind games, experience, magic of the psyche:
now you know it, now you don't.

Anyway, life gets harder—for Ernest
who can't sleep at night still seeing the lungs,
hassled by the trucker's family suing him
for wrongful death.

And John Henry still walks with a limp,
takes something for the pain, and doesn't get laid
much, now that it's all over.

Now that again it's all over.

ALL THAT RETURNS

Vegetation does grow back—
hillside scars, bomb craters, fill-in somewhat;
trees reach as high as ever
and monkey sounds are there again,
insect songs, calls of florid birds.

Mines have nearly all been cleared
one leg at a time

Women selling their black market lives
give smiles in return
and buy you Saigon tea

Pock-marked walls of old shrines
are filled and painted—no evidence
of war apparent in the walls, the faces
of worshippers, passers-by, the young

Yet that's not true: Look again, look closely, back
of their staring gaze where the wars still burn—
artillery overhead, airstrikes, the dull thud of a mortar round
landing in a fortified bunker, the stares merciless,
relentless as years, wars growing back
like leaves or limbs
vegetation burning behind their eyes.

HUNTING FOR ANTIQUES

I need parts for an old lamp
and another table. I love old tables,
the patina of worn wood, many layers of polish
showing the use and care of families
for generations: You can feel the years,
the lives, just running your hand
over the wood. But in a corner,
in an old shop display case,
I see medals, military decorations,
gathering dust, ribbons wrinkled, faded,
colors bleeding into one another
and the metal tarnished with years of neglect.
And I wonder how a family can give these up
knowing the soldier himself probably said,
as we all did, *A medal and a dime*
will get you a cup of coffee;
and so they are of no value; not as heirlooms,
as antiques, the measure of a man's life
lost in the war or not, it doesn't matter.
But they are given, as the Army says, because
men need to be rewarded for their sacrifice
and men wouldn't do what they do in war
without them—Yet I remember one soldier who saved
another wounded in the chest, by dragging
him back under heavy fire, getting wounded himself
and dying later from those wounds. And the medal
went home to his wife to be placed in a drawer
and after awhile never looked at again—
eventually to be found here, or someplace like here,
to be bought for a dime
and a story we have to make up
to go with each one.

TAKING YOUR ARM

It isn't
that I took
your arm
floating in the river
lightly

It wasn't your arm
anyway

I laughed
because it is the way
I have

Of reconciling
incongruities

For example,
remember
when the first
incoming rounds
pounded us into the dirt

And we said
it's just like the movies

Still, it was damned hard
to pull the pins
from grenades
with our teeth

And the flak—
black puffs of smoke
out there
past the line of the wings,
a carnival, a celebration
utterly removed from us

I watch it a lot now,
still making it through
almost
without a scratch

But the out-of-place, again,
the incongruities

Your arm, like that of a doll,
the elastic that kept all the members
together, cut, and there it is
floating in this water
that smells like black shit

Hey man,
I don't want to hear about it
I didn't see it
It wasn't your arm
I wasn't even there
I never saw anything
come on, I'll buy you a beer

MEMORIAL DAY, QUETICO, 1980

Where they got those 4-deuce mortars
we'll never know;
we'd hustled every cache
for a dozen klicks in every direction—
bulldozed every tunnel entrance
we could find—or blew it,
or salted it with gas.
The area was clear, defoliated,
patrolled, no action in more than a month—
all wildlife, all jungle sounds,
buried beneath that heavy smoke
hanging in free fire distance.

Every week we got our mail,
sand bags oozed sweat, our
jungle boots rotted and stank ...

Night jungle sounds descending—a few monkeys,
a strange bird pressing into the dark:
a soft *plop*, a few charges at best
and the earth fell apart, bunkers
torn into air and dirt, lifting out
with the soft sound of a ball
folding into the mitt—collapsing
as weightless as rain. Barrels
hottened and smoked, magazines piled
at our feet. As soon, they were gone,
air strike ineffective,
hanging the smell of burning oil
in our lungs ...

The *plop, plop* of frogs in a pond
softens the night—no charges.

A GOOD DAY

You wake in the morning
and it's rainy and cold

Your cat wants in, is scratching at the door—
you're glad it's back, although the night before
you screamed, "All right, go outside,
get run over you dumb fucker, see if I care!"

Your work isn't done—was due yesterday
or the day before;
all your good friends want to screw
your wife; she doesn't get up
until you're dressed and ready to go

Your eggs cook too long; your toast
is dry; the morning paper is wet
and peels off like burned skin

And this
is the best part of the day

Once, on your day off,
you started drinking at ten—
just a few, but enough to feel good;
you dug through an old trunk,
found the grenade you'd stolen years ago
from the only employer who ever liked your work,
and went out to the woods
you'd played in as a kid

It was almost fall, a few
trees just beginning to turn;
you pulled the pin, threw
it as hard as you could,
wrenching your arm as it wobbled
into the trees, off aim, bouncing back
against a branch before it
finally went off, exploding leaves
and dirt and forest debris
with a sound so loud
it rang in your ears all day.

Easily
the best day, of any,
in your entire life.

TO A FRIEND WHO STILL INSISTS ON WRITING ABOUT THE WAR

for W.D. Ehrhart

The war poet in you
just will not die—
lines run through your days
like tracers, marking your past,
searching out the targets of your hate:
the hypocrite, the liar, the bullshitter,
death wardens of assorted colors,
all hit with incendiary rounds until
they're just a jellied mass
the size of a scrawny chicken.
You haven't got the decency to stop
though others wish you'd go away
and write of how the light
shines through the trees
and other pretty things the decent
ones can read at tea.

In their niceness let them rot.
Here's some gun oil and a patch:
clean out the barrel of your weapon
and fire line after line
of copper-jacketed truth into every
ignorant bastard who puts his hand
on your shoulder and says, "Now, now,
take it easy, forget about it,
the war is over for us all."

FOR THE CAMERAS

A Kurdish rebel holds up the small,
bright-red dress of a young child,
the child disappeared, captured, killed or sold,
it doesn't matter—there are hundreds of dresses,
shirts, shoes half-buried in the dry, broken earth.

This is how I will measure my life—

The limp form of an infant lifted into a cart,
the mother's face, lovely and young, looking up
into the face of the sky, not a mark on her body—
a bloodless death, and so many: our guide trips
over battlefield debris, a metal canister, exploded,
now rusting to the earth.

This is how I will measure my life—
a few pages still readable in the broken stone
speak of lives once part of this place,
the place where no one may live,
old cemeteries bulldozed, fresh graves scattered
and hidden in the hills.

In a relocation camp
many miles away, crowds of old women
raise their arms above their heads,
like schoolchildren answering questions,
their fingers raised high and extended
to indicate how many of the family
are missing, and no one knows where—
the tyranny of memory, of loss, as despotic
as any regime. These women cry loss like a song,
tear at their faces, their clothes.

This is the ritual of our earth
measured grave by grave—and anyone with a VCR
can watch the proud footage of executions,
tortures, drugged interrogations—a head-slap,
an official firing a pistol
to administer the coup de grace
on bodies slumped to the ground,
hands tied behind to a post.

This is what I take with me measuring my life
blindfolded, hands tied behind, repeating
a last numbing request, knowing nothing
will change—
color of that dress fixed like a prayer,
like blood on this earth.

FOLLOW ME

Twenty years after
he'd lost an arm and an eye,
almost twenty years to the day
that he'd received a Silver Star
he went back to his last duty base,
ate lunch at the officers' mess
and listened politely to conversation
of other wars, cutbacks, lack of
promotions, and how the PX prices
were as high as what you could get
at a good discount store.

He listened, and when some Major in Finance
asked him where he'd spent his tour in Vietnam,
he told them near An Tuc where the blind side
of him had lived as vividly now as then
in lush jungle, luxuriant heat,
and the blinding flash that left him
unable to play catch with his son
or to see his way to the end of the war.

But the conversation was merely
military courtesy, and his dress blues,
the ribbons, even the Silver Star
did nothing to capture anyone's
attention amidst all that concern
for monthly pay and allowances:
And he allowed as much
returning to half the darkness he was born to
taking his pay as he'd always done
one long night at a time.

SHRAPNEL

That night we talked about the war
you drew a layout of your firebase,
lined out the azimuths of your 105's,
explained the days—12 on, 12 off,
with fire missions routine and plotted
as your games of chess: you sketched
the line where you dug in that night
the VC stormed your base—barrels lowered
to point blank range, flechettes shredding
earth and air, and Spooky ringing the base:
a crown of tracers rained cordons of red
as sappers overran the guns, blew cannons
belly up, and you exploded shadows
round after round throughout the night.

Too close, with this retelling,
you sat back silent,
reached out, crumpled the map,
choked back the tears of memory and rage,
and then, because grown men don't cry—
unless alone—you stood up, shaking,
and politely left the room.

CAMBODIA

His only job is to build shelves.
Each day he adds another, and another
to this makeshift shrine,
this library of discarded remains,
and each day they come
dumping his work in a pile outside his door.
His children sort out the skeletal parts,
put each bone in the right
pile for their father
who stacks the skulls neatly
on the shelves that he builds
for the men who come.

Sometimes, breaking the rhythmic monotony,
he talks to a few who strike him
with the strangeness of their vigilant grins
or the quizzical looks in their vacant, shadowy eyes;
and *his* eye measures the curve of a bone,
perhaps of the woman who had been his wife;
he smooths with his shirt
the rounded white blade of a rib
he might have traced with his hand long ago.

He holds a sun-whitened jaw up to the light,
uses a femur for a doorstop.
He believes in their teeth,
catalogs sun-cured wounds splintered and healed—
a scrap of cloth still adheres.

But the shelves ...
in this temple they almost build themselves,
pyramids of skulls stacking higher and higher
on this altar disappearing into the sky,
and no one,
not even the most terrible or wondrous of gods
can see their faces, or recognize their names.

FISHING FOR BASS

The sun slips low
and it's time

I push my canoe
out from shore—
a shallow inlet
strewn with fallen pines—
float on the flat
plane of water
over promising structure,
rocks piled like the rubble
of an old foundation,
a mammoth tree,
its girth so wide
a man could live inside

The wind has died down
and the sky clouds
with mosquitoes
the cloud gray
spinning like gritty factory smoke
above the canoe

Inhale and the lungs are filled,
the mouth:
I recall locusts one night in Missouri
in a small town outside an army base—
green wings caught
in the lamplight
flooding still air with luminous sound
whirring in hair and ears,
bitter green taste in the mouth—
town closed up for the night.

But here my hands bleed;
I pull a mosquito net over my face;
the net sucks in with each breath.

And bass rise
to the bait
gulp dozens in one lunge,
one break of the surface calm

And a large smallmouth takes my bait,
a plastic worm
that twists in its cavernous maw
as the fish leaps and leaps again
across the surface, against the cold white
face of the moon
catches like a sapper against the light
only here, across the black plain of this lake—
silhouettes of magnesium white and black—
the strike of a trip flare
floods the dark.

.

MARKING TIME

for Gerald McCarthy

Each day he wakes to a new
forgetting: this morning he caught the movement
of a squirrel rustling through the leaves;
the cold frost of this early hour ran up his back—
he froze and looked for signs of anything else
moving out of the corner of his eye.

Above the courthouse the black flag flies:
POW/MIA snapping in the wind.

He walks through towns he's never heard of,
streets empty, concrete cold, footsteps
echoing in the half-light.

He walks back and forth
in the tiger cage of American streets;
strips of shadow cut across his back;
the light cuts in and out
like a rubber hose raising welts
across the backs of his legs.

There are no mornings he wakes to,
the sun a bare light bulb
always on in the prison din
that is a constant, like distant gunfire,
that never ceases, noise and light the same.

You can see it in his eyes
when you look away, ashamed.

He moves on, walks into the unreadable past,
taps out the ciphers of his story
with each step.

MOUSSORGSKY, McGOVERN, PHILADELPHIA

This morning I read a poem about
Moussorgsky—that one piece—
Pictures At An Exhibition,
and now, in late afternoon,
I walk through a gallery
noting the latest Art Deco
resurgence—some slipping
back into the past, into art,
past art, past recidivism—
such a cute aesthetic ...

Years ago I stood on a corner in Philadelphia
and passed out leaflets to passers-by—
leaflets in front of the Academy of Music
where Moussorgsky would soon be
played to the enthrallment of
women wearing mink and ermine,
dyed sable and nutria: Their long cars
pulled up out front where they descended,
gracefully, politely, ignoring my exhortation:
See Senator McGovern, Monday, in Philadelphia ...
the day before the election—by then
even the war didn't matter—no guilt, no
apologies, but Moussorgsky, this concert
Friday afternoons for women
who wouldn't come to the city at night—
mink in the afternoon

And one polite lady, elegant, older,
says, "You're not really going
to vote for him, are you?" "Yes Ma'am":
She doesn't take the leaflet, but
she smiles—I say, "Enjoy the concert."
Moussorgsky—safe, Eugene Ormandy safe—
pictures at an exhibition—
and that rabid democrat, a ward leader,
had students holding photos
enlarged to 2X3 feet—the My Lai massacre—
"That will get their attention," he says,
"Women don't want to see that; they'll vote
for McGovern because of the blood, the babies."
More pictures, another Mercedes—

On Monday the streets are packed,
crowd push, hard even to breathe, to stay
on one's feet—Phil Ochs sings—some time,
before or later, he throws a basket of
fruit into a swimming pool, screaming
about the war, starvation, death—but he
could easily have sent them the fruit—he sang,
before McGovern spoke, and hanged himself
sometime later. Nixon Imperator Augustus: Let them
eat their dead

Art for art's sake, art for the sake of the
Republic—the Main Line—MLR—
main line of resistance, perimeters
choked with the dead: Romanticize history
and get away with it—art, pictures,
a symphony only the dead can hear,
and everyone, maybe, will live to tell of it,
saved for art, for war, for the foolish hell of it—
Moussorgsky dies in the traffic sounds—years later,
we write about nothing. Art for the era, the age
of art.

NIGHT AMBUSH II

Everyday he tells me
he's put the war behind him;
he doesn't watch the movies,
doesn't read the books.
The scars on his arm
are covered, always, even
on the hottest days of summer.

I tell him the story of my uncle,
a veteran of World War II
who fought on Okinawa;
he grew a beard to cover
the hollowed part of his
reconstructed chin and jaw
and went through life
with everyone thinking he was
eccentric, unshaven, and
they jokingly called him Abe,
never knowing his story,
never the least concerned.

Last night the fireflies were thick
in the backyard, points of light
like tiny explosions in the distance,
and we watched until the silence
crawled into our bones and slept,
like children we read to
story after story marking time
like tracers.

We have another beer and say good night;
he leaves the same way he came
with the same story.
I go upstairs, read a story to my
daughter, a story that ends strongly,
properly, with closure strong
as a door being shut
after the lights are turned off.
I turn on the hallway light
targeting the shadows in doorways,
go downstairs, have a last beer
before I close up the house for the night.

My daughter wakes awhile later,
says there's something under her bed—
I come up, say the darkness is her friend,
it lets her sleep and dream.
I tell her there is nothing there
as I lift the dust ruffle and look underneath.
I tell her there's nothing to be afraid of,
but I don't look into her questioning face
hoping she won't see, will never know,
that I'm still afraid of the dark.

INTERREGNUM

The age has ended. In light rain
Tumultuous crowds exult and frolic
While those closest to it all—their hearts
Seared by a dictatorial passion,
Their minds stained like the blade
Of a hunter's knife—
Feel the splayed final hours
Unravel and split.

The King has no clothes on.

Through years of long awakenings
To the pulse of hatred,
And insane righteousness
That preyed on its own thought
We have waited
Lungs filled with ice
Hands torn fleshless from frozen steel.

The age has ended.
Flickering shadows lengthen into night,
Die out in streets
Still filled at dawn.

BETTER DEAD THAN BORING

Bowling Green, 1984

This morning a Huey came in
over the campus trees
descended in a cordoned off area
near the Business Administration Building—
a show for the ROTC boys,
their sorority girls:
an impressive piece of equipment
spit shined and strac,
not even a fingerprint
on the pilot's black visor
reflecting the sun—
all that attention to detail

Details, candidate, details!
It's the little things that'll kill you,
the TAC officer said, over and over
like some Biblical quote ...

Yeah, I guess so,
like a small piece of shrapnel, no bigger
than a pin that entered the chest
under the arm, that found that one small
space in a flak jacket unprotected—it took
an hour to find the wound ...

I sleep late now, avoid as much of the day as I can,
but the *pock, pock, pock* of the blades
carving this early morning sky ...

Elegy, mimic of heartbeat,
song that quickens the blood;
the body shivers, sweats like cold metal ...

Lock and load coming over the trees
gunships prepping the treeline
the first ship down, recon by fire
a squad runs off to the left, another
lies prone in the tall grass, puts out
good cover to the front, two pigs raking the trees
tracers arcing low over the brush—
a door gunner walks fire
through a hootch, abandoned, rotting,
just in case—
another ship takes fire
a couple 79 rounds lift smoke into the trees
pinpoint a mortar crew, dug in
bracketing the LZ
another ship pulls off hit in the tail
each squad taking fire
gunships in and out of the trees—
another LZ two klicks away—
the only possibility—obvious, a set up
as other ships land, are hit by heavy fire—
Chicom 107's—Phantoms roll in at tree top level,
scream by, huge canisters tumbling
twin balls of flame, rolling orange-black smoke;
trees incinerate, oxygen sucked out of bunkers
leaving behind the smell of burning oil and flesh
     ...
There's the usual bitching about
the role of the university in military affairs
but hell, for some it's the only way out—
the only way out of a trailer park
on the edge of some cornfield—either that or be
a shit kicking farmer, or work for a potato chip
factory and come home smelling like overused grease—
better to die in Lebanon or Grenada than live in Ohio ...

I watch the ship lift into the air
drink coffee, do nothing
for the rest of the day

LONG AFTER THE WAR

Each morning he wakes
dreaming of his last love
and the one before
endlessly spiralling behind
out of reach
but so close in the warmth
of his bed, the hardness
he wakes to, of light,
mattress, pubis bone
some dim coupling
repeated like racial memory

Again, late in Asia, during the war
the woman light beneath,
he, balanced on fingertips and toes
the way he'd done push-ups
for years during high school wrestling,
and then reaching beneath,
placing one hand under
her waist and lifted to meet
bone to bone as she arched, pushed,
once, twice, three times hard
and sank back,
dropping the arch of her moist, smooth back

Now, ten or twenty push-ups at best—
and not on his fingertips either
and no nights of ten, twelve, thirteen or more
draining desire, turning to red,
the loosening hold

Now his hand tightens
as did hers, clenching, pulling down
as if gravity weren't enough
to work against in the pure artistry
of form moving through this dark space coupling time
and room, love splitting the cells,
careening as undiscovered particles
through reaches and reaches of light, love,
all past years of love
again with each waking.

AT THE CRASH SITE OF A B-52: JANUARY 1994

for H. Bruce Franklin

When the Americans come back
they search for artifacts
the way Europeans once excavated the ruins
of Tra-kiêu or Mi-so'n or Tham Khuyen.
They sift earth still black
from the fires of war: jet fuel
and ammunition that burned
all day, all night, so long ago—
sift through a fine screen
until they find a Seiko watch,
its world-time dial unable
to tell the time anywhere
in any city in this world.
They find a major's insignia,
a piece of velcro, some metal pitted,
corroded, burned beyond recognition
and a few slivers of bone.
They dig deeper, screen more bone,
but the bones of a child:
the mother remembers, knows the major,
the captain, the sergeant are all buried with her son—
she recognizes the bones of her son
the way she imagines the major's
mother would recognize hers, if she let go,
if she let her son sink into the earth
that is beginning again to smell like soil
that will grow things, the way it did before,
if she'd just let go, if she'd only learn
that war is not something you come back from
whether you were killed or not, that the resurrection
is only a story for the gods—that a candle,
the perfume of burning incense, a flower
growing from the garden of this blackened earth
brings more than a lasting peace, more
than a mother can hope for.

HOW IT ENDS

After Nam he dumped his fatigues
in a laundry bag and threw them
in the basement. His boots went
down separately to mildew, to lose
their consummate spit shine
for which he had been famous
and been promoted out of Basic to PFC.

But he wore his faded field jacket
across campus, let his hair grow long
enough almost to cover his rank,
and little by little the cuffs frayed,
his name tag came loose at the corner
and was pulled off, unit designations
were ripped off after too many beers
followed by too many shots.

And he found himself the enemy once again,
targeted as crazy by the administration
when he blocked access to the Registrar,
considered useless by professors
who didn't like his hard questions
in class, challenging their authority.

And when someone stole it hanging on
a coat rack in a bar, he just yelled, *Fuck it!*
having been ripped off so many times by the war
it was second nature, as tight fitting as his skin
and he was no more cold without it
walking naked down drunken American streets.

TEACHING THE WAR

I read a poem about the war
in Vietnam to my class, most of them young
and unscarred by any element of history;
and for them Vietnam might as well be
the Peloponnesian War, or Caesar's
conquering of Gaul. But this one
student, a girl, a Hmong refugee
who escaped from the KR, the Vietnamese,
old enemies and the new, her own countrymen—
she winces and pulls back, a strategic
withdrawal from the poem that wounds
worse than a fragmentation grenade,
and I talk to her after class, coaxing
her to tell the story of escaping
to the border camps in Thailand,
braving it all, evading the AK's,
the killing fields, losing a sister
who gave herself up—a decoy or diversion—
sacrificing herself for her family
who went free to bribe their way,
according to ancient custom,
all the way to here.

She tells me some of what she saw,
at times looking away, out the window
as if her words could break free
and fly from her, never to return—
reflections borne far away
never again to trouble her face.
Remembering slowly, she describes more of what she saw
of the Vietnamese occupation, and I ask her,
Didn't your mother warn you about the Vietnamese?
And she looks at me as if I'd pulled all
past enmity skeletoned in the closet
out for everyone to see like dirty pictures:
Yes, she says, *She did; she often told us stories,
and warned us: all our nights filled with warning.*

FRIENDS

How strange
these long years after,
your bodies risen into myth,
metal fires burned out at last,
debris pushed into the sea,
and all that death for nothing
but a few stories as recompense,
as titillation—and would you believe?
(*remember that?*) there are those who wish they'd
joined you—seen the gunship downed,
the fuelship blown up on the pad,
body parts strung out like ornaments,
who wish they'd gone and gotten a few themselves—
I'll bring you back an ear, they'd say.
Friends, a fool's rain falls
and falls upon your sinking graves.

SHOULDERS

for CPT Paul Bowman, KIA VN, 1969

Before you went
we sat at the bar in the Officers' Club
and drank and talked—you said the EOD
course wasn't challenging enough, the war
was going badly, many mistakes were being made.
We talked of tactics till our minds wore out
and then of women—not breasts or legs—not
the common concerns of those lieutenants
sitting over there eyeing that pretty waitress.
We talked of shoulders
and the smooth line that went down the eye
the way that last farewell liqueur
went down our throats. Then two weeks later
you were dead—a letter said it all.
I've hated mail the long years since.
I still love a woman's shoulders—
I watch them always, always;
and some nights when I lie with my wife,
I curl my hands around her shoulders and pull tight—
and see your hands, your heart and lung all shot away,
and somewhere, shoulders, shivering.

WILD RASPBERRIES

This is the usual jaunt—
the sun still low
and the smell of night air
still lingers, gives way
to the warmth of this field, in this light:
wild raspberries ripen;
I grab handfuls for breakfast,
walk along the tree line, listen to
the sounds of the world, feel its movement.
My daughter hangs back, watches a grasshopper
leap and fly; she follows; it leaps again
and again she follows, her eyes filled
with the wonders of the world.
I watch and recall the eyes of a child
born to the war, the darkness of her stare,
almost eyeless yet there after all these years,
all the fatigue of daily battles, skirmishes
no one ever wins. She comes toward me,
a dangerous gift in her hand.
It is the blessing of war—
what comes after—that she brings.

TAPS

Girl Scouts, even the younger Brownies, play Taps
after each meeting, repeating the ritual
around a campfire late at night
before returning to their musty tents,
singing, *Day is done, Gone the sun ...
All is well, Safely rest, God is nigh*;
and I'm startled by my six year old daughter
singing to this music that I remember,
and remember again as each day is done.

When she inadvertently watches a scene
from a war movie with soldiers in dress blues
surrounding a casket draped with the flag,
she says, hearing the men play Taps,
"How do *they* know that song?"

And I pray to all the gods who ever
interfered in the lives, the wars, of men
never to have her know that music
other than around the fire toasting marshmallows,
making s'mores, singing this last song
before a night of rest, never to feel the chill
up and down the spine, the holding back of all
that's brought back with those strains
to men who will never know rest.

NOTES ON THE POEMS

BIEN HOA, 1968

A standard ploy of drill sergeants to exact compliance with a rule requiring trainees to change their boots every day was to have one of the two pairs of boots issued to a soldier painted with white dots above the heel. Each day in morning formation the NCOs could easily check to see that the same pair of boots was not worn two days in a row.

GB

In the United States arsenal of chemical weapons, GB and VX are the standard nerve agents. GB (Sarin) is an organophosphate; its chemical composition is isopropylmethyl fluorophosphonate. GB works as a cholinesterase inhibitor; its antidote is atropine. The practical demonstration described in the poem took place at Ft. McClellan Alabama. As part of the training students of chemical warfare were schooled in the use of an atropine auto-injector to counter the effects of nerve agents. In this case the demonstration proved only that such counter measures do not always work.

In March of 1969 in Skull Valley, Utah, near Dugway Proving Ground, some 6,000 sheep died as the result of some errant chemical warfare tests conducted by the U.S. Army. The sheep exhibited most of the classic symptoms of exposure to nerve agents, but despite the admission that the Army had conducted tests the day before, the Army denied responsibility.

Biblical scripture contains numerous references to the sacrificing of sheep. The complete epigraph to the poem, from the book of Isaiah, is as follows:

> And behold joy and gladness, slaying oxen, and killing sheep, eating flesh and drinking wine: let us eat and drink; for tomorrow we shall die.

PATAYA BEACH R&R, 1968
Pataya Beach is on the Gulf of Siam. 1968 was the year of the monkey.

BOUNDARY WATERS and MEMORIAL DAY, QUETICO, 1980
Large tracts of lake country have been set aside in northern Minnesota and Ontario for wilderness canoeing and camping. On the American side this wilderness area is known as the Boundary Waters Canoe Area; on the Canadian side this area is Quetico Provincial Park.

MARKING TIME
The tragic irony of the POW/MIA issue, aside from the political manipulations that have prevented reestablishing diplomatic relations with Vietnam, is that many thousands of veterans have been incarcerated in the U.S. while thousands of others are imprisoned within their own psychologies adversely affected by the Vietnam War.

MOUSSORGSKY, McGOVERN, PHILADELPHIA
Eugene Ormandy was reputed by critics to have kept the Philadelphia Orchestra respectable, but not exceptional; performing the Moussorgsky piece, a rather common and predictable selection, typifies the rather safe, comfortable programs the orchestra presented in those years. Phil Ochs was a popular folk singer in the '60's who wrote and performed anti-war songs including "I Ain't Marching Anymore." He sang before Senator McGovern appeared at a large rally in Philadelphia the day before the 1972 election. The Main Line extends from the city to the affluent suburbs of Philadelphia.

AT THE CRASH SITE OF A B-52, JANUARY 1994
Mi-so'n, Tra Kiêu and Tham Khuyen are archaeological sites in Vietnam. Tra-Kiêu and Mi-so'n contain Cham art and inscriptions dating from the 4th and 7th centuries respectively. The cave at Tham Khuyen has yielded remains of Homo Erectus.

TEACHING THE WAR
After the Khmer Rouge had systematically exterminated more than a million of their countrymen, the military forces of Vietnam moved into Cambodia and occupied that country for ten years, until 1989. The United States condemned this occupation as cultural genocide, and, in one of the great ironies of the Indochina war, the United States supported the Khmer Rouge in their fight against the Vietnamese.

FRIENDS
"Would you believe?" was a line used by Don Adams (Maxwell Smart, Agent 86) on the T.V. series *Get Smart*. The line was repeated frequently by NCOs and training officers as part of the standard process of harassing trainees and subordinates. The sentiment expressed by that line was especially appropriate since it gauged the distance between the fanciful or absurd and the actual, a distinction blurred often by the war in Vietnam.

TAPS
A girl scout tradition, "s'mores" are treats made at night while sitting around the campfire. Toasted marshmallows and chocolate bars are sandwiched between squares of graham crackers.